DRAGON
IN THE
WOODSHED

A Collection of Poetry

SELECTED AND ARRANGED BY
John O'Leary

Scholarstown Educational Publishers Ltd. London

Introduction

Dragon in the Woodshed is an exciting collection which should appeal to every nine to ten year old. The exercises which accompany many of the poems are designed to encourage creativity and to explore, at an elementary level, the rudiments of poetic language. References to art, drama and music further encourage this process.

The 'Easy-Learn' poems, found in each section, are self-explanatory, and 'Poetry Extra' is an added bonus for a teacher or pupil who wishes to supplement the themes presented.

John O'Leary

ISBN 1 85276 030 3

Editor: Francis Connolly

Illustrations by Rosemary Bradshaw

Printed by Folens Publishing Co. Dublin 24

© 1988 — Scholarstown Educational Publishers Ltd. London

Contents

Round the Corner, Past the Wall

Mist and Moonlight

Acknowledgements

The publishers wish to thank the following for permission to include copyright material in the collection:

"John Mouldy" by Walter de la Mare by permission of The Literary Trustees of Walter de la Mare and the Society of Authors as their representative: "White Fields", "Check", "In the Orchard" by permission of the Society of Authors on behalf of the copyright owners, Mrs. Iris Wise; "The Magical Mouse" by Kenneth Patchen from *Collected Poems* by permission of New Direction Publishing Corporation; "The Visitor", "The Witch's Cat", "Anne and the Fieldmouse" by Ian Serraillier, © 1963 Ian Serraillier, and Oxford University Press; "Television Aerials" by Stanley Cook from *Come Along: Poems for Young Children* by Stanley Cook by permission of the author; "There Came a Day", "Woodpecker" by permission of Faber and Faber Ltd. from *(a) Season Songs (b) Under The North Star* by Ted Hughes; "The Song the Train Sang" by Neil Adams by permission of the author; "The Marrog" by R.C. Scriven by permission of the author; "Alone in the Grange" by Gregory Harrison by permission of the author; "The Mystery Creatures" by Wes Magee by permission of the author; "Sir Winter" by Jean Kenword by permission of the author; "My Gerbil" by John Kitching by permission of the author; "The Intruder" by James Reeves, © James Reeves Estate, reprinted by permission of the James Reeves Estate; "Spring Song", "We Wouldn't Change Him" from *Stirabout Lane* by J.D. Sheridan by permission of J.M. Dent & Sons Ltd.; "Lizzie and the Apple Tree" by Julie Holder from *A Third Poetry Book* compiled by John Foster published by Oxford University Press; "Waiting at the Window" by A.A. Milne from *Now We Are Six* by permission of Methuen Children's Books; "The Hippopotamus's Birthday" by E.V. Rieu from *The Flattered Flying Fish And Other Poems* by permission of Methuen & Co.; "I'm Alone in the Evening", "The Hidebehind" by Michael Rosen from *Mind Your Own Business* by permission of Andre Deutsch; "I Like Soft Boiled Eggs", "My name is Supermouse" by John Kitching by permission of the author.

In the case of some copyright material the publishers have been unable to contact the copyright holders. We will be glad to make the usual arrangements with them should they contact the publishers.

WIDE AWAKE INSIDE

Waking

My secret way of waking
Is like a place
to hide.
I'm very still,
my eyes are shut.
They all think I am sleeping
but
I'm wide awake inside.

They all think I am sleeping
but
I'm wiggling my toes.
I feel sun-fingers
on my cheek.
I hear voices whisper-speak.
I squeeze my eyes
to keep them shut
so they will think I'm sleeping
BUT
I'm really wide awake inside
— and no one knows!

Lilian Moore

Waiting at the Window

These are my two drops of rain
Waiting on the window-pane.

I am waiting here to see
Which the winning one will be.

Both of them have different names.
One is John and one is James.

All the best and all the worst
Comes from which of them is first.

James has just begun to ooze.
He's the one I want the lose.

John is waiting to begin.
He's the one I want to win.

James is going slowly on.
Something sort of sticks to John.

John is moving off at last.
James is going pretty fast.

John is rushing down the pane.
James is going slow again.

James has met a sort of smear.
John is getting very near.

Is he going fast enough?
(James has found a piece of fluff.)

John has hurried quickly by.
(James was talking to a fly.)

John is there, and John has won!
Look! I told you! Here's the sun!

A. A. Milne

INVENT 5 UNUSUAL GAMES FOR INDOORS ON RAINY DAYS

WHAT POSSIBLE PRIZE COULD YOU GIVE JOHN THE RAINDROP? MAYBE A DAMP SPONGE! THINK UP 5 OTHER PRIZES.

BORED SILLY HANDICAP
DRAW UP 10 RUNNERS FOR THE RACE OF THE YEAR
EVERY NAME MUST INCLUDE AN OBJECT IN YOUR HOUSE.
e.g. 1. FIREPLACE FANCY
2. COAL SCUTTLE

First Day at School

A millionbillionwillion miles from home
Waiting for the bell to go, (to go where?)
Why are they all so big, other children?
So noisy? So much at home they
must have been born in uniform
Lived all their lives in playgrounds
Spent the years inventing games
that don't let me in. Games
that are rough, that swallow you up.

And the railings.
All around, the railings.
Are they to keep out wolves and monsters?
Things that carry off and eat children?
Things you don't take sweets from?
Perhaps they're to stop us getting out
Running away from the lessins. Lessin.
What does a lessin look like?
Sounds small and slimy.
They keep them in glassrooms.
Whole rooms made out of glass. Imagine.

I wish I could remember my name
Mummy said it would come in useful
Like wellies. When there's puddles.
Lellowwellies. I wish she was here.
I think my name is sewn on somewhere
Perhaps the teacher will read it for me.
Tea-cher. The one who makes the tea.

Roger Mc Gough

Poetry *Nothing To Do* by Shel Silverstein, *Looking Down On Roofs* by Marian
Extra Lines, *Bonfire* by Jean Kenward.

Dog in the Playground

Dog in the playground
Suddenly there.
Smile on his face,
Tail in the air.

Dog in the playground
Bit of a fuss:
I know that dog —
Lives next to us!

Dog in the playground:
Oh, no he don't.
He'll come with me,
You see if he won't.

The word gets round;
The crowd gets bigger.
His name's Bob.
It ain't — it's Trigger.

They call him Archie!
They call him Frank!
Lives by the Fish Shop!
Lives up the Bank!
Who told you that?
Pipe down! Shut up!
I know that dog
Since he was a pup.

Dog in the playground:
We'll catch him, Miss.
Leave it to us.
Just watch this!

Dog in the playground
What a to-do!
Thirty-five children,
Caretaker too,
Chasing the dog,
Chasing each other.
I know that dog —
He's our dog's brother!

Allan Ahlberg

1. Name three birds that visit the playground.
2. Pair each creature in A with the correct activity in B.

A	B
dog snoozing by the fire	annoyed and angry
dog chasing a cat	ashamed and unhappy
dog carrying a paper	excited and high-spirited
dog snapping at a bee	pleased and proud
dog when you scold it	happy and at ease

2. Make up a conversation between a sparrow and a rook arguing about a crust of bread in the school yard. Begin like this:

Sparrow: It's mine, I saw it first!
Rook: You saw it first but I'm bigger than you!

1. Make a scraffito drawing based on this poem.

The Chair

A funny thing about a Chair:
You hardly ever think it's *there*.
To know a Chair is really it,
You sometimes have to go and sit.

Theodore Roethke

Poetry *First Day At School* by Roger McGough, *Kidnapped* by Shel Silverstein,
Extra *Scissors* by Allan Ahlberg.

Shining Things

I love all shining things —
  The lovely moon
The silver stars at night,
  gold sun at noon,
A glowing rainbow in
a stormy sky,
Or bright clouds hurrying
  when the wind goes by.
I love the glow-worm's elf-light
in the lane,
And leaves a-shine with glistening
drops of rain,
The glinting wings of bees,
  and butterflies,
My purring pussy's green
  and shining eyes.
I love the street-lamps shining
  through the gloom,
Tall candles lighted in
  a shadowy room,
New-tumbled chestnuts from
  the chestnut tree,
And gleaming fairy bubbles
  blown by me.
I love the shining buttons
  on my coat,
I love the bright beads round
  my mother's throat,
I love the coppery flames
  of red and gold,
That cheer and comfort me
  when I'm a-cold.
The beauty of all shining things
  is yours and mine.

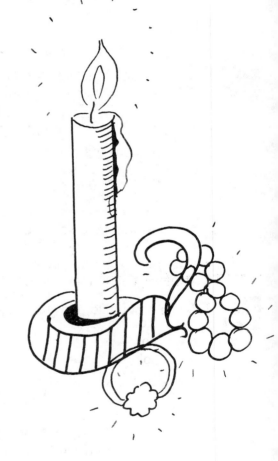

Elizabeth Gould

Summer Goes

Summer goes, summer goes
Like the sand between my toes
When the waves go out.
That's how summer pulls away,
Leaves me standing here today,
Waiting for the school bus.

Summer brought, summer brought
All the frogs that I have caught,
Frogging at the pond,
Hot dogs, flowers, shells and rocks,
Postcards in my postcard box —
Places far away.

Summer took, summer took
All the lessons in my book,
Blew them far away.
I forgot the things I knew —
Arithmetic and spelling too,
Never thought about them.

Summer's gone, summer's gone —
Fall and winter coming on,
Frosty in the morning.
Here's the school bus right on time.
I'm not really sad that I'm
Going back to school.

Russell Hoban

Out of School

Four o'clock strikes,
There's a rising hum,
Then the doors fly open,
The children come.

With a wild cat-call
And a hop-scotch hop
And a bouncing ball
And a whirling top,

Grazing of knees,
A hair-pull and a slap,
A hitched up satchel,
A pulled down cap,

Bully boys reeling off,
Hurt ones squealing off,
Aviators wheeling off,
Mousy ones stealing off,

Woollen gloves for chilblains,
Cotton rags for snufflers,
Pigtails, coat-tails,
Tails of mufflers,

Machine gun cries,
A kennelful of snarlings,
A hurricane of leaves,
A treeful of starlings,

Thinning away now
By some and some,
Thinning away, away,
All gone home.

Hal Summers

1. Join the words in A to the correct description in B.

A	B
shadows	shoot out the school door
clouds	sinks in the west
the sun	fly in the wind
children	sail across the sky
papers	run across the grass

2. Put each phrase below into a sentence.
   (a) *cried with sadness*   (b) *laughed with delight*
   (c) *squealed with excitement*   (d) *moaned with pain*
   (d) *shrieked with fear*

3. Divide your day into words! Describe each part with one word.

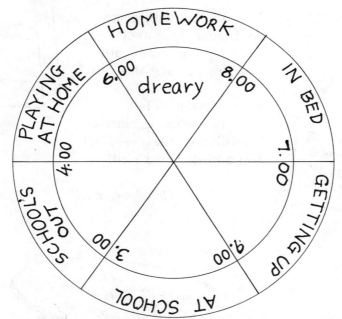

 Use a cardboard box to make a model of the school. Use stand-up cut-out figures to represent children.

 Listen to the 'Overture' from *William Tell* by Rossini.

Poetry *School 's Out* by W. H. Davies, *Picking Teams* by Allan Ahlberg, *Hurry*
Extra *Home* by Leonard Clark, *No Swimming in the Town* by Ian Serraillier, *Another Day* by John Cunliffe.

Skateboarder

I can soar, I can swoop,
I can buckle at will,
I've tried looping the loop,
I've touched fifty downhill.

I've done end-over-end,
I've shot into the sky,
I zoom down, then ascend,
Gravity I defy.

I am flirting with death
As I hang there in space,
I am holding my breath
For I'm winning this race.

I am moving so fast
That my vision is blurred.
I am flying at last —
I'm a bird! I'm a bird!

Charles Connell

 Listen to 'March' from *Children's Games* by George Bizet.

Poetry Extra   *The Fifteen Acres* by James Stephens, *Dancin'* by Roger McGough, *The Runners* by Allan Ahlberg, *Transportation Problem* by Richard Armour.

My Shadow

I have a little shadow that goes in and out with me.
And what can be the use of him is more than I can see.
He is very, very like me from the heels up to the head.
And I see him jump before me when I jump into my bed.

The funniest thing about him is the way he likes to grow...
Not at all like proper children, which is always very slow:
For he sometimes shoots up taller, like an India-rubber ball,
And he sometimes gets so little that there's none of him at all.

One morning very early, before the sun was up,
I rose and found the shining dew on every buttercup:
But my lazy little shadow, like an arrant sleepy-head,
Had stayed at home behind me and was fast asleep in bed.

Robert Louis Stevenson

I Like Soft-Boiled Eggs

I like soft-boiled eggs.
I like liver.
I like chicken legs
And jelly. See it shiver.

I like cabbage —
All kinds of greens.
I like sausages
And bubbling brown baked beans.

John Kitching

I'm Alone in the Evening

I'm alone in the evening
when the family sits
reading and sleeping,
and I watch the fire in close
to see flame goblins
wriggling out of their caves
for the evening

Later I'm alone
when the bath has gone cold around me
and I have put my foot
beneath the cold tap
where it can dribble
through valleys between my toes
out across the white plain of my foot
and bibble bibble into the sea

I'm alone
when mum's switched out the light
my head against the pillow
listening to ca thump ca thump
in the middle of my ears.
It's my heart.

Michael Rosen

1. Describe five imaginary things you see when you look into a fire.
2. What do the following things you see in the house look like?
   (a) *water-tap*   (b) *light-bulb*   (c) *teapot*   (d) *fire-tongs*
   e.g. *A light-switch looks like a bird's beak.*
3. Make lists of words to describe each of the following,
   (a) eating e.g. *munching*
   (b) talking e.g. *chattering*
   (c) drinking e.g. *gulping*
4. The *Darklin* lives in your attic. What does it look like?

1. Write a **Haiku** about bedtime. A **Haiku** has three lines of different lengths.
   Here is an example:

I am now resting ← —————— **5 syllables**
night stills as cars shush beyond ← —————— **7 syllables**
my small heart beating ← —————— **5 syllables**

Listen to *Eine Kleine Nacht Musik* by Mozart.

Bedtime

When I go upstairs to bed,
I usually give a loud cough.
This is to scare The Monster off.

When I come to my room,
I usually slam the door right back.
This is to squash The Man in Black
Who sometimes hides there.

Nor do I walk to the bed,
But usually run and jump instead.
This is to stop The Hand —
Which is under there all right —
From grabbing my ankles.

Allan Ahlberg

**Poetry
Extra** *The Sounds In The Evening* by Eleanor Farjeon, *The Grebs* by Mike Harding, *Nightmare* by Siv Widerberg, *What Someone Said When He was Spanked On the Day Before His Birthday* by John Ciardi.

The Attack

When I have settled down in bed
And pulled the sheets over my head,

I know that I am safe inside
And from Red Indians can hide,

Who by their hawk-eyed chief are sent
To gallop round and round my tent

Bareback upon their stallions,
Whooping loud and firing guns

All across the rolling plain
Out of sight and back again.

But when I come up for some air
There are redskins everywhere,

On the warpath, near my head,
Circling round and round the bed,

And then I hide myself until
They have gone and all is still.

Leonard Clark

LITTLE CREATURES EVERYWHERE

Little Things

Little things that run and quail
And die in silence and despair;

Little things that fight and fail
And fall on earth and sea and air;

All trapped and frightened little things
The mouse, the coney, hear our prayer.

As we forgive those done to us,
The lamb, the linnet, and the hare,

Forgive us all our trespasses,
Little creatures everywhere.

James Stephens

21

The Wire-Haired Fox-Terrier

I am a blithe
   Fox Terrier
And nobody can be
   Merrier
   Or friskier
   Or whiskrier
Or should that be whisKERRier?
Than a wire-haired
   Fox Terrier
I am a great
   Cat catcher
And garden tennisball
   Racer
   Nosey parker
   Noisy barker
And middle of the lawn bone-burier
I'm a wire-haired
   Fox Terrier.

I am a rough
   Rat worrier
And bouncing scoot and
   Scurrier
   Out of mischief
   Into mischief
Stream-paddler and stick-carrier
I'm a wire-haired
   Fox Terrier.
At night I am
   A sleeper
And nobody can sleep
   Deeper
   Or snoozier
   Or cosier
When the frost outside gets frozier
Than a tired
   Fox Terrier.

Leslie Norris

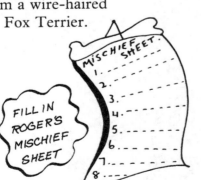

Poetry *Roger the Dog* by Ted Hughes, *Lone Dog* by Irene McLeod, *My Puppy* by
Extra   Aileen Fisher, *A Dog On The Beach* by John Walsh.

Lone Dog

I'm a lean dog, a keen dog, a wild dog, and lone;
I'm a rough dog, a tough dog, hunting on my own;
I'm a bad dog, a mad dog, teasing silly sheep;
I love to sit and bay the moon, to keep fat souls from sleep.

I'll never be a lap dog, licking dirty feet,
A sleek dog, a meek dog, cringing for my meat;
Not for me the fireside, the well-filled plate,
But shut door, and sharp stone, and cuff, and kick, and hate.

Not for me the other dogs, running by my side;
Some have run a short while, but none of them would bide;
O mine is still the lone trail, the hard trail, the best,
Wide wind, and wild stars, and the hunger of the quest!

Irene R. McLeod

Duck's Ditty

All along the backwater,
Through the rushes tall,
Ducks are a-dabbling,
Up tails all!

Ducks' tails drakes' tails,
Yellow feet a-quiver,
Yellow bills all out of sight
Busy in the river!

Slushy green undergrowth
Where the roach swim —
Here we keep our larder,
Cool and full and dim!

Every one for what he likes!
We like to be
Heads down, tails up,
Dabbling free!

High in the blue above
Swifts whirl and call —
We are down a-dabbling
Up tails all!

Kenneth Grahame

Anne and the Fieldmouse

We found a mouse in the chalk quarry today
In a circle of stones and empty oil drums
By the fag end of a fire. There had been
A picnic there: he must have been after the crumbs.

Jane saw him first, a flicker of brown fur
In and out of the charred wood and chalk-white.
I saw him last, but not till we'd turned up
Every stone and surprised him into flight,

Though not far — little zigzag spurts from stone
To stone. Once, as he lurked in his hiding-place,
I saw his beady eyes uplifted to mine.
I'd never seen such terror in so small a face.

I watched, amazed and guilty. Beside us suddenly
A heavy pheasant whirred up from the ground,
Scaring us all; and, before we knew it, the mouse
had broken cover, skimming away without a sound,

Melting into the nettles. We didn't go
Till I'd chalked in capitals on a rusty can:
THERE'S A MOUSE IN THOSE NETTLES. LEAVE
HIM ALONE. NOVEMBER 15TH ANNE.

Iar Serraillier

1. What did Jane see first?
2. How did the fieldmouse move from stone to stone?
3. How did Anne know it was frightened?
4. Why was Anne amazed and guilty, do you think?
5. How did the fieldmouse escape?
6. Name five things you might find dumped in an old quarry.

1. Draw the front page of *The Daily Nibble* newspaper in your
   copy, and tell the exciting story of the fieldmouse's escape.

Make chalk-pictures of Anne and the fieldmouse.

Poetry *The House Mouse* by Jack Prelutsky, *The Mouse in the Wainscot* by Ian
Extra   Serraillier, *The Mouse* by Elizabeth Coatsworth, *Mice* by Rose Flyeman.

My Gerbil

Once I had a gerbil —
Bought me by my Dad
I used to watch it in its cage,
Running round like mad
Or sleeping in a corner
Nesting in a hole
Made of shavings, bits of wool
And chewed up toilet roll.

I kept it in the kitchen
In the cage my cousin made.
It flicked all bits out on the floor
Mum grumbled — but it stayed.
I fed it; gave it water;
Was going to buy a wheel.
I used to take it out sometimes —
To stroke. I liked the feel —
All soft, with needle eyes,
A little throbbing chest.
I'd had a bird, a hamster too:
The gerbil I liked best.

I came downstairs one morning.
I always came down first.
In the cage there was no movement.
At once I knew the worst.
He lay there in the corner.
He'd never once been ill —
But now, fur frozen, spiky,
No throbbing, eye quite still.

I tell you — I just stood there
And quietly cried and cried,
And, when my Mum and Dad came down,
I said, 'My gerbil's died'.

And still I kept on crying,
Cried all the way to school,
But soon stopped when I got there
They'd all call me a fool.

I dawdled home that evening.
There, waiting, was my mother.
Said: 'Would you like another one?'
But I'll never want another.

John Kitching

1. What things do gerbils like to eat?
2. Make a list of five 'gerbil-words', e.g. *twitching*.
3. How do we know that the person in the poem loved the gerbil?
4. Which words tell us that the gerbil was dead?

Write a Shape-Poem inside a pet mouse drawn in your copy.
Here are some words to help you.

Make a cage for a gerbil using pipe-cleaners and soft wire.
You can make a gerbil from plasticine.

Poetry *Mr. Tortoise* by E. Pope, *Goldfish* by John Walsh, *What On Earth Do They*
Extra *Think About?* by John D. Sheridan, *The Christening* by A. A. Milne.

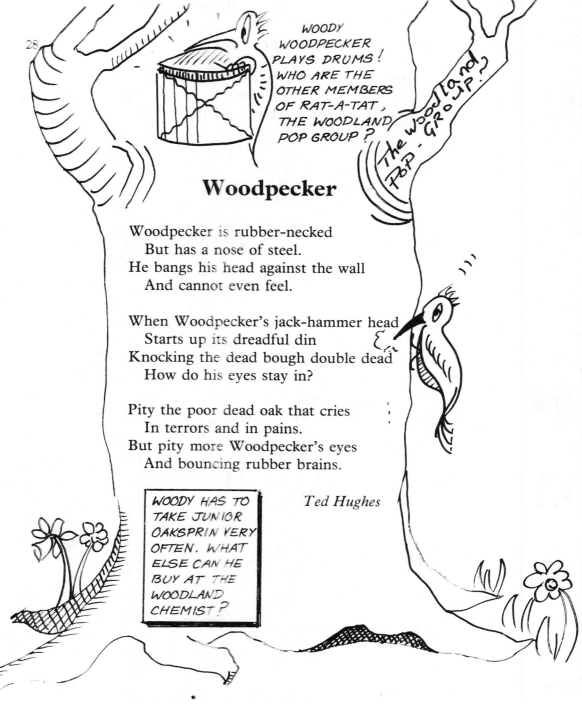

28

WOODY WOODPECKER PLAYS DRUMS! WHO ARE THE OTHER MEMBERS OF RAT-A-TAT, THE WOODLAND POP GROUP?

The Woodland Pop-Group?

Woodpecker

Woodpecker is rubber-necked
    But has a nose of steel.
He bangs his head against the wall
    And cannot even feel.

When Woodpecker's jack-hammer head
    Starts up its dreadful din
Knocking the dead bough double dead
    How do his eyes stay in?

Pity the poor dead oak that cries
    In terrors and in pains.
But pity more Woodpecker's eyes
    And bouncing rubber brains.

Ted Hughes

WOODY HAS TO TAKE JUNIOR OAKSPRIN VERY OFTEN. WHAT ELSE CAN HE BUY AT THE WOODLAND CHEMIST?

Make a large wall-frieze of the woodpecker on a tree.

Poetry Extra   *The Blackbird* by Humbert Wolfe, *The Woodpecker* by Richard Church, *Robin* by Iain Crichton Smith, *Little Trotty Wagtail* by John Clare.

The Donkey

I saw a donkey
  One day old,
His head was too big
  For his neck to hold.

His legs were shaky
  And long and loose;
They rocked and staggered
  And weren't much use.

He tried to gambol
  And frisk a bit,
But he wasn't sure
  Of the trick of it.

His queer little coat
  Was soft and gray,
And curled at his neck
  In a lovely way.

His face was wistful,
  And left no doubt
That he felt life needed
  Some thinking out.

So he blundered round
  In venturous quest,
And then lay flat
  On the ground to rest.

He looked so little
  And weak and slim,
I prayed the world
  Might be good to him.

Elizabeth Shane

Geoffrey

— Geoffrey? Geoffrey?
She peers into the night:

— Come on puss, come on Geoffrey?
I do hope he's all right.

But deep, deep in the shadows
He's a beast without a name.
With claws of steel and bloody fangs
He moves like a flickering flame.

Silently down the alley
Silently round the shed
Until he explodes in a fire-spitting blur
With a shriek to wake the dead.

And a tawny savage strikes again
With a speed too quick for sight,
And the bleeding vanquished visitor
Yowls off into the night.

— Geoffrey! There's my Geoffrey!
Ah, look at him lick his paw!
Who's my lovely boy then?
— What's that red stuff round his jaw?

And the beast stares back unblinking
With eyes that are blank and bright
As Geoffrey, king of the alleys,
Waits for tomorrow night.

Andrew Davies

1. Does Geoffrey hear his owner calling him?
2. Which words and phrases describe Geoffrey's anger?
3. What colour is he?
4. How do you know that he is a good fighter?
5. Is Geoffrey fond of his owner?

1. Make up a 'Wanted — Dead or Alive' poster.

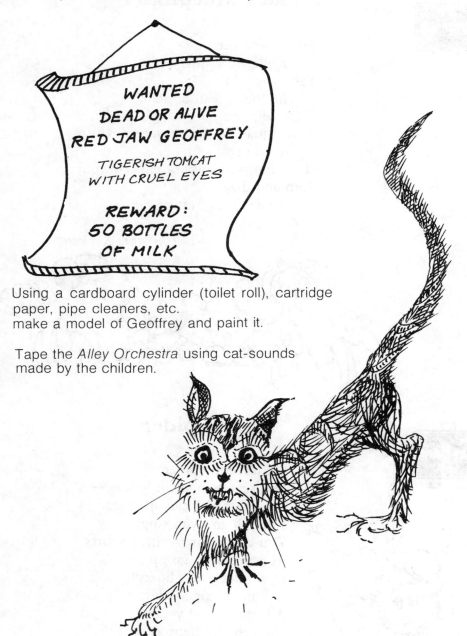

WANTED
DEAD OR ALIVE
RED JAW GEOFFREY

TIGERISH TOMCAT
WITH CRUEL EYES

REWARD:
50 BOTTLES
OF MILK

Using a cardboard cylinder (toilet roll), cartridge paper, pipe cleaners, etc. make a model of Geoffrey and paint it.

Tape the *Alley Orchestra* using cat-sounds made by the children.

Poetry   *The Tom-Cat* by Don Marquis, *Cleaning Ladies* by Kit Wright, *Five Eyes* by
Extra   Walter de la Mare, *Our Cats* by Wes Magee.

The Caterpillar

Brown and furry
Caterpillar in a hurry,
Take your walk
To the shady leaf, or stalk,
  Or what not,
Which may be the chosen spot.
  No toad spy you,
Hovering bird of prey pass by you;
Spin and die,
To live again as butterfly.

Christina Rossetti

Spider

Spider, Sir Spider,
You're a wonderful fellow —
On a thread I can spy there
You fall and you stop;
You come down with a scurry
And then you go up
In as much of a hurry!
O Spider, Sir Spider,
All brown and yellow,
On a thread light as air,
Where you fall and you stop,
You're a wonderful fellow!

Padraic Colum

IN BETWEEN ARE THE PEOPLE

The Intruder

Two-boots in the forest walks,
Pushing through the bracken stalks.

Vanishing like a puff of smoke,
Nimbletail flies up the oak.

Longears helter-skelter shoots
Into his house among the roots.

At work upon the highest bark,
Tapperbill knocks off to hark.

Painted-wings through sun and shade
Flounces off along the glade.

Not a creature lingers by,
When clumping Two-boots comes to pry.

James Reeves

Sing a Song of People

Sing a song of people
Walking fast or slow;
People in the city,
Up and down they go.

People on the sidewalk,
People on the bus;
People passing, passing,
In back and front of us.
People on the subway
Underneath the ground;
People riding taxis
Round and round and round.

People with their hats on,
Going in the doors;
People with umbrellas
When it rains and pours.
People in tall buildings
And in stores below;
Riding elevators
Up and down they go.

People walking singly,
People in a crowd;
People saying nothing,
People talking loud.
People laughing, smiling,
Grumpy people too;
People who just hurry
And never look at you.

Sing a song of people
Who like to come and go;
Sing of city people
You see but never know!

Lois Lenski

1. Where do people go
   (a) to see a film?
   (b) to see a play?
   (c) to have a meal?
   (d) to look at paintings?

2. Pair the people with the countries they come from:

   Holland   Swiss
   Switzerland   Dutch
   U.S.S.R.   Danish
   Denmark   Russian

3. Find five action words to go with each of the following words:
   (a) hands   (b) legs   (c) mouth   (d) eyes

Make up your own poem about children. Begin like this:

> *Sing a song of children*
> *Coming home from school . . .*

Make a collage of photographs from newspapers and magazines.

Some One

Some one came knocking
At my wee small door;
Some one came knocking,
I'm sure-sure-sure;
I listened, I opened,
I looked to left and right,
But nought there was a-stirring
In the still dark night;
Only the busy beetle
Tap-tapping in the wall,
Only from the forest
The screech-owl's call,
Only the cricket whistling
While the dewdrops fall,
So I know not who came knocking,
At all, at all, at all.

Walter de la Mare

Poetry
Extra   *Conjuror* by Clive Sansom, *The Vet* by Guy Boas, *Aunts and Uncles* by Mervyn Peake, *Newspaper* by Alan Horrox, *Picnic* by Hugh Lofting.

Alone in the Grange

Strange,
Strange,
Is the little old man
Who lives in the Grange.
Old,
Old;
And they say that he keeps
A box full of gold.
Bowed,
Bowed,
Is his thin little back
That once was so proud.
Soft,
Soft,

Are his steps as he climbs
The stairs to the loft.
Black,
Black,
Is the old shuttered house.
Does he sleep on a sack?

They say he does magic,
That he can cast spells,
That he prowls round the garden
Listening for bells;
That he watches for strangers,
Hates every soul,
And peers with his dark eye
Through the keyhole.

I wonder, I wonder,
As I lie in my bed,
Whether he sleeps with his hat on his head?
Is he really magician
With altar of stone,
Or a lonely old gentleman
Left on his own?

Gregory Harrison

1. Where does the little old man live?
2. Where do you think he keeps his box of gold?
3. What colour is his house?
4. Does he sleep on a sack or on a bed, do you think?
5. Why does he prowl around his garden?
6. Do you think he is a magician?
7. Tell why you would like to meet this little old man.

1. Match each word in List A with a word in list B.

A	B
little	narrow
bowed	looks
peers	small
strange	unusual
thin	bent

2. The old man's name is Bob. Use the Name-Stairs to make words that describe Bob.

Bald
   O..
     B....

1. Make a poster for your classroom entitled *Man or Magician*.

Monday's Child

Monday's child is fair of face,
Tuesday's child is full of grace,
Wednesday's child is full of woe,
Thursday's child has far to go,
Friday's child is loving and giving,
Saturday's child works hard for a living,
But the child that is born on the Sabbath day
Is bonny, and blithe, and good, and gay.

Poetry Extra *Dan the Watchman* by John D. Sheridan, *When We Go Over To My Grandad's* by Michael Rosen, *My Uncle Dan* by Ted Hughes, *Giant Denny* by Derek Stuart.

We Wouldn't Change Him

Mary is tidy, Mary is neat,
From the top of her head to the soles of her feet;
She learns her lessons and knows her 'spells',
She seldom fights, and she never yells.
But Tom!
Tom is untidy
From Monday to Friday,
And when we scrub him on Saturday night
It takes us an hour to get him white.
He gets mud on his knees, and mud on his nose,
Mud on his boots, and mud on his clothes.
He walks into every puddle he sees,
Tears his trousers on roadside trees,
Fills his pockets with little frogs,
And sits on his hunkers to talk to stray dogs.
And yet, if you know any nice little lad,
Who's always good, and who's never bad,
Who knows his tables, and learns his 'spells',
And never gives Red Indian yells —
We won't exchange.
Isn't it strange?
We'd rather have Tom with his freckled face
Than anyone else in curls and lace.
He may leave mud
On the mats in the hall,
But we wouldn't change him,
At all, at all.

John D. Sheridan

The People

The ants are walking under the ground,
And the pigeons are flying over the steeple,
And in between are the people.

Elizabeth Madox Roberts

The Mystery Creatures

They dwell on a planet not far
    from the Sun.
Some fly through the sky, while
    others just run.
Some have big heads which are
    hairless as tin,
while others have hair which
    sprouts from their skin.
They dig food from dirt, and
    gobble dead meat.
The young squeal like pigs if you
    tickle their feet.
They slurp, burp, and grunt;
    their manners are bad.
Their eyes become waterfalls
    When they feel sad.
Well, who are these creatures?
    Can you guess who?
The answer is easy: it's you,
you, and YOU.

Wes Magee

1. Who are the mystery creatures?
2. Name five ways by which people travel long distances.
3. Write one word which means *hairless as tin.*
4. Name five vegetables grown by farmers.
5. What should mannerly children say if they slurp or grunt while eating?
6. Fill in the missing letters:
   A waterfall of t___s fell from Linda's eyes.

Make up a short rhyme, using the names of boys and girls you know. Here is an example:

> *Michael, David, Pauline, Dora,*
> *Jason, Joseph, Eileen, Nora.*

1. Make a silhouette painting based on the poem.
2. Organize a drama with children miming the creatures described in the poem while the rest of the class recite it.

Poetry *The Alien* by Julie Holder, *Intelligence Test* by Vernon Scannell, *The*
Extra *Intruder* by James Reeves, *Man the Musicmaker* by Roger McGough.

Lizzie and the Apple Tree

Once upon a time,
Every day for a while,
Lizzie sat up in the apple tree
Behind the leaves
And a smile.

And she said when they called
That she wouldn't come down
Till the apples dropped off
And the leaves turned brown.

She swung her legs
And laughed at their frown
And didn't come down
Didn't come down.

Lizzie sat up in
The apple tree's hair
In the wind and the rain
In the sun and the air.

Lizzie swung in
the apple tree's arms
And ignored her family's
Tempers and charms.

When Lizzie turned into an apple
They ceased to scold and berate
her
And when the apples fell down
They forgot she was Lizzie —
And ate her!

Julie Holder

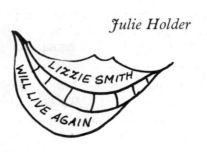

MAKE YOUR OWN
LIZZIE STICKERS
WITH SLOGANS LIKE
" SAVE LIZZIE SMITH "
" LIZZIE YOU'RE NO PEACH "
" LIZZIE YOU'RE THE
APPLE OF MY
EYE "

NO POET SHOULD BE ALLOWED TO TURN A PERSON INTO AN APPLE

GOVERNMENT HEALTH WARNING
APPLES ARE HUMAN TOO!

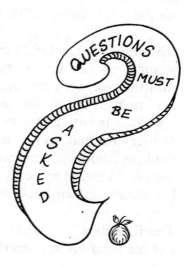

QUESTIONS MUST BE ASKED

1. Make a mosaic using coloured paper torn into small pieces. Draw an outline of Lizzie in the apple tree, and paste on the coloured paper.
2. Form a *Save Lizzie Smith Club* in your class. Make badges, stickers, etc.

Poetry *Adventures of Isabel* by Ogden Nash, *Veruca Salt* by Roald Dahl,
Extra *Adventures of Little Katy* by Carolyn Wells, *The Cure* by Alfred Noyes.

Hungry Mungry

Hungry Mungry sat at supper,
Took his knife and spoon and fork.
Ate a bowl of mushroom soup, ate a slice of roasted pork,
Ate a dozen stewed tomatoes, twenty-seven deviled eggs,
Fifteen shrimps, nine baked potatoes,
Thirty-two fried chicken legs,
A shank of lamb, a boiled ham,
Two bowls of grits, some black-eye peas,
Four chocolate shakes, eight angel cakes,
Nine custard pies with Muenster cheese,
Ten pots of tea, and after he
Had eaten all that he was able,
He poured some broth on the tablecloth
And ate the kitchen table.

His parents said, 'Oh Hungry Mungry, stop these silly jokes.'
Mungry opened up his mouth, and 'Gulp,' he ate his folks.
And then he went and ate his house, all the bricks and wood,
And then he ate up all the people in the neighbourhood.
Up came twenty angry policemen shouting, 'Stop and cease.'
Mungry opened up his mouth and 'Gulp,' he ate the police.
Soldiers came with tanks and guns.
Said Mungry, 'They can't harm me.'
He just smiled and licked his lips and ate the U.S. Army.

The President sent all his bombers — Mungry still was calm,
Put his head back, gulped the planes, and gobbled up the bomb.

He ate his town and ate the city — ate and ate and ate —
And then he said, 'I think I'll eat the whole United States.'

And so he ate Chicago first and munched the Water Tower,
And then he chewed on Pittsburgh but he found it rather sour.
He ate New York and Tennessee, and all of Boston town,

Then he drank the Mississippi River just to wash it down.
And when he'd eaten every state, each puppy, boy and girl
He wiped his mouth upon his sleeve and went to eat the world.

He ate the Egypt pyramids and every church in Rome,
And all the grass in Africa and all the ice in Nome.
He ate each hill in green Brazil and then to make things worse
He decided for dessert he'd eat the universe.

He started with the moon and stars and soon as he was done
He gulped the clouds, he sipped the wind and gobbled up the sun.
Then sitting there in the cold dark air,
He started to nibble his feet,
Then his legs, then his hips
Till he sat there just gnashin' his teeth
'Cause nothin' was nothin' was
Nothin' was nothin' was
Nothin' was left to eat.

Shel Silverstein

1. Why was Hungry Mungry so hungry?
2. What do you think he ate for his breakfast?
3. How many kinds of meat did he gobble down?
4. How many cities did he eat?
5. Name two foreign countries mentioned in the poem.

1. Make up five crazy sandwiches,
   e.g. *ice-cube sandwiches*
2. Make up ten names like *Hungry Mungry*. Use the following words — *Happy, Thirsty, Sleepy, Dozy, Moany, Meany, Pokey, Speedy, Smiley, Saddy.*
3. You are the chef in the Hungry Mungry Restaurant. Write a menu using the names of Irish towns,
   e.g. *Fried Dublin with Galway Car-parks*

1. Using cut-outs and toy items such as false teeth, spoons, knives, forks, bowls etc., you can make a big display in the classroom of all the things Hungry Mungry ate.
2. Organize a drama called *The Hungry Mungry Supper Show*. Use can be made of the objects collected in (1). One child is chosen to play Hungry Mungry. As he calls for his food, other children bring it to him.

Poetry *Dunderbeck* (Anon), *Giant Jojo* by Michael Rosen, *Bones* by Walter de
Extra la Mare, *Mr Skinner* by N. M. Bodecker.

The Watchmaker's Shop

A street in our town
  Has a queer little shop
With tumble-down walls
  And a thatch on the top;
And all the wee windows
  With crookedy panes
Are shining and winking
  With watches and chains.

(All sorts and all sizes
  In silver and gold.
And brass ones and tin ones
  And the new ones and old;
And clocks for the kitchen
  And clocks for the hall.
High ones and low ones
  And wag-at-the-wall.)

The watchmaker sits
  On a long-legged seat
And bids you the time
  Of the day when you meet;
And round and about him
  There's ticketty-tock
From the tiniest watch
  To the grandfather clock.

I wonder he doesn't
  Get tired of the chime
And all the clocks ticking
  And telling the time;
But there he goes winding
  Lest any should stop,
This queer little man
  In the watchmaker's shop.

Anon

A DRAGON IN THE WOODSHED

The Marrog

My desk's at the back of the class
And nobody nobody knows
I'm a Marrog from Mars
With a body of brass
And seventeen fingers and toes.
Wouldn't they shriek if they knew
I've three eyes at the back of my head
And my hair is bright purple
My nose is deep blue
And my teeth are half yellow half red?
My five arms are silver with knives on them
    sharper than spears.
I could go back right now if I liked —
And return in a million light years.
I could gobble them all for
I'm seven foot tall
And I'm breathing green flames from my ears.
Wouldn't they yell if they knew
If they guessed that a Marrog was here?
Ha-ha they haven't a clue —
Or wouldn't they tremble with fear!
Look, look, a Marrog
They'd all scream — and SMACK.
The blackboard would fall and the ceiling would crack
And the teacher would faint I suppose.
But I grin to myself sitting right at the back
And nobody nobody knows.

R. C. Scriven

45

A Small Dragon

I've found a small dragon in the woodshed
Think it must have come from deep inside a forest
because it's damp and green and leaves
are still reflecting in its eyes.

I fed it on many things, tried grass,
the roots of stars, hazel-nut and dandelion,
but it stared up at me as if to say, I need
foods you can't provide.

It made a nest among the coal,
not unlike a bird's but larger,
it is out of place here
and is quite silent.

If you believed in it I would come
hurrying to your house to let you share my wonder,
but I want instead to see
if you yourself will pass this way.

Brian Patten

1. Why did the small dragon go into the woodshed?
2. What colour are its eyes, do you think?
3. Why did it not eat the food it got?
4. Name some places a dragon might like to make its nest.
5. Make up five *Rules of the House* for pet dragons.
   e.g. *No smoking in bed.*

1. What things could you buy in Cinderworth's Dragon Supermarket?
   Here are two — *shredded firelighters, torch bars!*
2. Make up a nursery rhyme or a lullaby for a baby dragon. Begin like this,

> *Hushaby hotbreath*
> *On the red coals...*

Make an egg-carton collage of the dragon on a sheet of strong cardboard or cartridge paper. Buttons can be used for its eyes and cotton wool as smoke from its nostrils.

Poetry Extra *Lost and Found* by Lilian Moore, *The Crocodile's Toothbrush* by Shel Silverstein, *The Sick Young Dragon,* by Derek Stuart, *Jocelyn, My Dragon* by Colin West.

Bear in There

There's a Polar Bear
In our Frigidaire —
He likes it 'cause it's cold in there.
With his seat in the meat
And his face in the fish
And his big hairy paws
In the buttery dish,
He's nibbling the noodles,
He's munching the rice,
He's slurping the soda,
He's licking the ice.
And he lets out a roar
If you open the door.
And it gives me a scare
To know he's in there —
That Polary Bear
In our Frigitydaire.

Shel Silverstein

 Paint or draw a picture of the bear in the Frigidaire. Collect the pictures in a book or art folder entitled *Bear in Here*

Poetry Extra *The Cow* by Roald Dahl, *Under My Bed* by Barbara Ireson, *The Wild Hog* (anon), *The Plug-Hole Man* by Carey Blyton.

My Dinosaur's Day in the Park

My pet dinosaur got in trouble
When we went for a walk in the park.
I took off his leash and let him run free.
He didn't come back until dark.

He ate up the new row of oak trees
(The gardener was fit to be tied).
Then he stopped in the playground and bent down his head
And the kids used his neck for a slide.

He knocked down the fence by the boat pond
With a swing of his twenty-foot tail;
When he stopped to explain he was sorry,
His legs blocked the bicycle trail.

When the sun set, my dino got worried;
He's always been scared of the dark.
He sat down on the ground and started to cry,
His tears flooded out the whole park.

A friend of mine rowed his boat over
When he heard my pet dino's sad roar
He showed him the way home to my house
And helped him unlock the front door.

He's a lovable, lumbering fellow
But after my pet had his spree,
They put up a sign in the park and it reads

NO DINOS ALLOWED TO RUN FREE

Elizabeth Winthrop Mahoney

1. Make up three long dinosaur names. Here is one — *Spell*asticky*word*osaurus Rex. Here is another — *Call*yourpetdogosaurus Rex!
2. Name five other trees the dinosaur ate?
3. Which words would you use to describe this dinosaur?
   (a) *troublesome*   (b) *polite*   (c) *savage*   (d) *kind*
4. Where did the pet dinosaur sleep when at home, do you think?

Make a list of jobs your pet dinosaur could do.
Here are two:
(a) *eating rubbish dumps*
(b) *protecting small children from bullies.*

Make out a 'NO DINOS ALLOWED TO RUN FREE' poster and display it in the classroom.

Poetry   *I Had a Hippopotamus* by Patrick Barrington, *Oliphaunt* by J. R. R. Tolkien,
Extra   *Eletelephony* by Laura E. Richards, *Advice to Children* by Carolyn Wells

The Hippopotamus's Birthday

He has opened all his parcels
        but the largest and the last;
His hopes are at their highest
        and his heart is beating fast.
O happy Hippopotamus,
        what lovely gift is here?
He cuts the string. The world stands still.
        A pair of boots appear!

O little Hippopotamus,
        the sorrows of the small!
He dropped two tears to mingle
        with the flowing Senegal;
And the 'Thank you' that he uttered
        was the saddest ever heard
In the Senegambian jungle
     from the mouth of beast or bird.

E. V. Rieu

The Silver Fish

While fishing in the blue lagoon,
I caught a lovely silver fish,
And he spoke to me, 'My boy,' quoth he,
'Please set me free and I'll grant your wish:
A kingdom of wisdom? A palace of gold?
Or all the fancies your mind can hold?
And I said, 'OK', and I set him free,
But he laughed at me as he swam away,
And left me whispering my wish
Into a silent sea.

Today I caught that fish again
(That lovely silver prince of fishes),
And once again he offered me,
If I would only set him free,
Any one of a number of wishes
If I would throw him back to the fishes.

He was delicious.

Shel Silverstein

1. Put in the correct sea-creature in each case:
   (a) *as flat as a* ....
   (b) *as big as a* ....
   (c) *as leggy as a* ....
   (d) *as soft as a* ....
   (e) *as tiny as a* ....
   (f) *as slow as a* ....

   | crab |
   | whale |
   | turtle |
   | sprat |
   | jellyfish |
   | plaice |

2. You have been swallowed by a shark. What three wishes will you grant the shark if he sets you free?

Paint an outline of the Silver Fish and let it dry. Cover the outline with a clear adhesive, and then sprinkle on some loose glitter. If you haven't got glitter, paste on some tinfoil instead.

Listen to 'Theme and Variations' from the *Trout Quintet* by Franz Schubert

Poetry Extra *The Silent Eye* by Ted Hughes, *The Owl and the Pussycat* by Edward Lear, *The Walrus and the Carpenter* by Lewis Carroll, *The Shark* by Lalla Ward, *The Flattered Flying Fish* by E. V. Rieu

The Magical Mouse

WRITE A JOB LIST
FOR A HOUSE MOUSE
1. COLLECT CRUMBS
UNDER THE
TABLE

I am the magical mouse
I don't eat cheese
I eat sunsets
And the tops of trees

I don't wear fur

I wear funnels
Of lost ships and the weather
That's under dead leaves
I am the magical mouse

I don't fear cats

Or woodowls
I do as I please
Always
I don't eat crusts
I am the magical mouse
I eat
Little birds and maidens
That taste like dust

WRITE OUT A MIGHTY MOUSE MENU

Mighty Mouse Inn Menu

SUPPORT YOUR LOCAL MOUSE. WRITE IN MOUSE WORDS

MINI MOUSE

MOUSE IS WONDERFUL

MAKE MOUSE STICKERS WITH SLOGANS

Kenneth Patchen

 1. Organize a drama entitled *The Magical Mouse Restaurant.* The restaurant manager, waiters, waitresses etc. to be played by children suitably dressed. Other children to act as customers who ask for most unusual dishes.

 2. Listen to *A Midsummer Night's Dream Overture* by Mendelssohn.

Poetry *A Monstrous Mouse* by X. J. Kennedy, *I Wish* by Lilian Moore, *Sky in the Pie*
Extra by Roger McGough, *The Visitor* by Jack Prelutsky

My Name is Supermouse

My name is Supermouse
I live in a Superhouse
I do as I please
I eat Supercheese
I chase Superrats
And I frighten nine lives
Out of all Supercats.

John Kitching

So Big!

The dinosaur, an ancient beast,
I'm told, was very large.
His eyes were big as billiard balls,
His stomach, a garage.
He had a huge and humping back,
A neck as long as Friday.
I'm glad he lived so long ago
And didn't live in my day!

Max Fatchen

The Fairies

Up the airy mountain,
  Down the rushy glen,
We daren't go a-hunting
  For fear of little men;
Wee folk, good folk,
  Trooping all together;
Green jacket, red cap,
  And white owl's feather!

Down along the rocky shore
  Some make their home;
They live on crispy pancakes
  Of yellow tide-foam;
Some in the reeds
  Of the black mountain lake,
With frogs for their watch-dogs,
  All night awake.

By the craggy hill-side,
  Through the mosses bare,
They have planted thorn-trees
  For pleasure here and there,
Is any man so daring
  As dig them up in spite,
He shall find the thornies set
  In his bed at night.

Up the airy mountain,
  Down the rushy glen,
We daren't go a-hunting
  For fear of little men;
Wee folk, good folk,
  Trooping all together;
Green jacket, red cap,
  And white owl's feather!

William Allingham

1. Where do the fairies live?
2. What do the fairies eat?
3. What do they use frogs for?
4. Why do they plant thorn trees?
5. Name five wild flowers the fairies plant for pleasure.

1. Play the Fairy Crossword Game. You will need a sheet of 1 cm. squared paper. You can work down, or from left to right. Fit in as many words as possible from the list provided. Begin with the word 'LEPRECHAUN'.

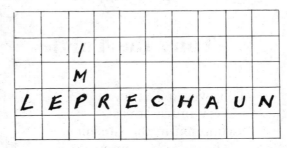

ELF
GOBLIN
FAIRY
TROLL
OGRE
IMP

PIXY
SPRITE
GNOME
BROWNIE
GREMLIN
LEPRECHAUN

Write your favourite verse into a copybook and decorate it with pictures of fairies.

Listen to 'The Fairy Garden' from the *Mother Goose Suite* by Ravel and *Mairséail Rí Laoise* (Ceolteoirí Chualainn)

Poetry Extra *Overheard on a Saltmarsh* by Harold Munro, *The Stolen Child* by W. B. Yeats, *Fairy Story* by Stevie Smith, *O, Here it is! and There it is!* by Mervyn Peake.

Tony the Turtle

Tony was a Turtle,
 Very much at ease,
Swimming in the sunshine
 Through the summer seas,
And feeding on the fishes
Irrespective of their wishes,
With a 'By your leave' and 'Thank you'
 And a gentlemanly squeeze.

Tony was a Turtle
 Who loved a civil phrase;
Anxious and obliging,
 Sensitive to praise.
And to hint that he was snappy
Made him thoroughly unhappy;
For Tony was a Turtle
 With most engaging ways.

Tony was a Turtle
 Who thought, before he fed,
Of other people's comfort,
 And as he ate them said:
'If I seem a little grumpy,
It is *not* that you are lumpy.'
For Tony was a Turtle
 Delicately bred.

E. V. Rieu

SEASON SONGS

Hallowe'en

At Hallowe'en some children are mean,
— But I'm not keen on being mean!
They throw stinkbombs in your houses,
A thing I'd never do.
I prefer to dress up and go to visit you.
I rush up to my mum's room
And her wardrobe fling open wide,
Lots of shapes and sizes tumble from inside;
Furry things, shiny things, belts and bows,
Delicate tights — all different colours,
For my darling toes.
Will I be Lady in Red or maybe in Black instead?
Now for a hat — Oh, I fancy that!
It's a top hat.
A knock on the door,
A creak on the floor,
Here come my friends to join me,
One is a robber, one is a cat,
And I am me, I'm sure of that.
Off we go in the darkness
Our bags crinkling,
Stars above are winking
On Hallowe'en Night.

Áine Casey, age 9

Beech Leaves

In autumn down the beechwood path
The leaves lie thick upon the ground.
It's there I love to kick my way
And hear the crisp and crashing sound.

I am a giant, and my steps
Echo and thunder to the sky.
How small the creatures of the woods
Must quake and cower as I pass by!

This brave and merry noise I make
In summer also when I stride
Down to the shining, pebbly sea
And kick the frothing waves aside.

James Reeves

1. When are the leaves thickest on the ground?
   (a) in August
   (b) in September
   (c) in October
2. Name the colours of the autumn leaves.
3. Which of these trees lose their leaves in autumn?
   (a) sycamore   (b) chestnut   (c) holly   (d) ash
4. Find the meanings of the following words:
   (a) crisp   (b) quake   (c) cower   (d) stride
5. Which words best describe the person in the poem?
   (a) happy   (b) cruel   (c) excited   (d) tired

1. Fill in the correct word in each case.
   (a) I . . . . . down to the shining, pebbly sea.
   (b) I . . . . into the narrow, gloomy cave.
   (c) I . . . . through the thorny, muddy field
   (d) I . . . . . . from the lowest, safest branch.

   > dangle
   > struggle
   > wriggle
   > stride

2. Draw a large leaf on a sheet of paper. Write a poem about autumn, using your own words. Each line has only one word, but the last line may have as many as you like.
   e.g.

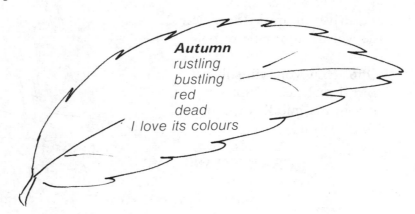

> **Autumn**
> *rustling*
> *bustling*
> *red*
> *dead*
> *I love its colours*

1. Make mobiles of cut-out leaf shapes. Hang them from a coat-hanger in the classroom.
2. Collect leaves and use them for printing, rubbings, stencil-designs or patterns.

Poetry *Leaves* by Ted Hughes, *Autumn Woods* by James S. Tippett and *Sweet*
Extra   *Chestnuts* by John Walsh, *Late Autumn Poem* by Roger McGough.

Sir Winter

I heard Sir Winter coming.
He crept out of his bed
and rubbed his thin and freezing hands:
'I'll soon be up!' he said.

'I'll shudder at the keyhole
and rattle at the door,
I'll strip the trees of all their leaves
and strew them on the floor;

'I'll harden every puddle
that Autumn thinks is his —
I'll lay a sparkling quilt of snow
on everything that is!

'I'll bring a load of darkness
as large as any coal,
and drive my husky dogs across
the world, from pole to pole.

'Oho! How you will shiver!'
And then I heard him say:
'But in the middle of it all
I'll give you

CHRISTMAS DAY!'

Jean Kenward

1. How long did Sir Winter spend in bed?
2. Where do you think he lives?
3. What will he do to the trees?
4. How will Sir Winter harden every puddle?
5. How does he travel from pole to pole?
6. What nice present does Sir Winter give to everybody?
7. Find the meanings of these words:
   (a) shudder   (b) strew   (c) quilt

1. Make up words using the letters of 'WINTER':

Wet
Ice
N
T
E
R

2 Write your own poem about winter. Begin like this:

> *O, please, Sir Winter, stay away,*
> *I fear your freezing fingers . . .*

 Make a frieze based on winter.

 Listen to 'Winter Scene' and 'Waltz of the Snowflakes' from *The Nutcracker Suite* by Tchaikovsky.

Christmas is Coming

Christmas is coming,
  The geese are getting fat,
Please to put a penny
  In the old man's hat.
If you haven't got a penny,
  A ha'penny will do;
If you haven't got a ha'penny,
  Then God bless you!

Poetry *Week Of Winter Weather* by Wes Magee, *Winter Report* by Lilian Moore
Extra   and *White Fields* by James Stephens.

The Friendly Beasts

Jesus our brother, kind and good,
Was humbly born in a stable rude,
And the friendly beasts around him stood;
Jesus our brother, kind and good.

'I,' said the donkey, shaggy and brown,
'I carried his mother up hill and down,
I carried her safely to Bethlehem town;
I,' said the donkey, shaggy and brown.

'I,' said the cow, all white and red,
'I gave him my manger for his bed,
I gave him my hay to pillow his head;
I,' said the cow, all white and red.

'I,' said the sheep, with the curly horn,
'I gave him my wool for his blanket warm;
He wore my coat on Christmas morn.
I,' said the sheep with the curly horn.

'I,' said the dove, from the rafters high,
'cooed him to sleep, my mate and I,
We cooed him to sleep, my mate and I;
I,' said the dove, from the rafters high.

And every beast, by some good spell,
In the stable dark, was glad to tell,
Of the gift he gave Emmanuel,
The gift he gave Emmanuel.

Anon.

Make this poem part of a Christmas drama which you can tape using carols and sound effects.

Paint the Story of Christmas on your classroom windows.

The Carol-Singers

Last night the carol-singers came
   When I had gone to bed,
Upon the crisp white path outside
   I heard them softly tread.

I sat upright to listen, for
   I knew they came to tell
Of all the things that happened on
   The very first Noël.

Upon my ceiling flickering
   I saw their lantern glow,
And then they sang their carols sweet
   Of Christmas long ago.

And when at last they went away,
   Their carol-singing done,
There was a little boy who wished
   They'd only just begun.

Margaret G. Rhodes

Poetry Extra *A Stormy Night One Christmas Day* by Michael Rosen, *My Christmas List* by Gyles Brandreth, *Snowflake Souffle* by X. J. Kennedy.

Springburst

(Please read this from the bottom)

FLOWER!
the
slowly   slowly
the *petal* curling
the *bud,*
awakening,
Oh, the
up!
straight
I know!
Now
hm.
hm
see.   see.
me   Hm   me
Let   Let
higher . . .
must reach
for the sky —
Now, must reach
I be!
I live!
up
tip
warmth
coolness
water,
food and
life growing,
life, being,
in the dark —
(seed style)
spark
A

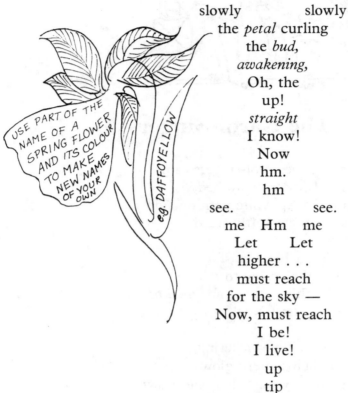

USE PART OF THE NAME OF A SPRING FLOWER AND ITS COLOUR TO MAKE NEW NAMES OF YOUR OWN

e.g. DAFFOYELLOW

WHAT DID THE DAFFODIL SAY TO THE FROG?

MAKE UP YOUR OWN SPRING WORDS e.g. SPRING-CHATTER

MAKE UP A SPRING MENU FOR HEDGEHOGS

John Travers Moore

Spring Song

There is going to be a dance,
  I can feel it in the air —
  What kind of frock will the daffodil wear?
  Gold for the sun and green for the clover;
  Spring is on the way
  And the winter's nearly over.

A soft little wind
Out behind the hill
is practising tunes
For the shy daffodil.
He daren't start yet
To play with all his might;
He daren't start yet,
For the time isn't right;
He daren't start yet,
For the frocks aren't made,
And the fairy needles flash
In the green forest glade.
Green thread, gold thread, laughing all together —
Heigh for the dance and the bright spring weather.

John D. Sheridan

1. Make a spring-flower collage using rolled, coloured tissue paper.
2. Make a seed-collage. You will need a grass seed, mustard seed, cress seed, etc. Also wallpaper paste and a sheet of cardboard.

Listen to *On Hearing the First Cuckoo in Spring* by Delius.

Poetry *Seed Song* by Christopher Rowe, *It Was Spring In The Fields* by Michael
Extra Rosen, *April* by Ted Robinson, *Spring Song* by William Blake.

Summer Song

By the sand between my toes,
By the waves behind my ears,
By the sunburn on my nose, .
By the little salty tears
That make rainbows in the sun
When I squeeze my eyes and run,
By the way the seagulls screech,
Guess where I am? *At the . . .!*
By the way the children shout
Guess what happened? *School is . . .!*
By the way I sing this song
Guess if summer lasts too long:
You must answer Right or . . .!

John Ciardi

1. How old is the child in the poem, do you think?
2. Write down the names of the months you spend on summer holidays.
3. Which words best describe the child in the poem?
   (a) busy   (b) excited   (c) happy   (d) lazy
4. Write down the colours of the rainbow.
5 Make a list of five 'seaside' words. Each word must have the letter 's',
   e.g. *sudsy, sparkling.*

Make up a **Haiku** about summer. A **Haiku** has three lines of different lengths.
Here is an example:

A sunny morning
sparrows bathing dry feathers
in cool ponds of dust

2. Fill the beach ball with seaside words.

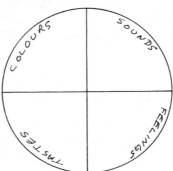

The Boy's Song

EASY-LEARN

Where the pools are bright and deep,
Where the grey trout lies asleep,
Up the river and o'er the lea —
That's the way for Billy and me.

Where the blackbird sings the latest,
Where the hawthorn blooms the sweetest,
Where the nestlings chirp and flee —
That's the way for Billy and me.

Where the mowers mow the cleanest,
Where the hay lies thick and greenest,
There to trace the homeward bee —
That's the way for Billy and me.

Where the hazel bank is steepest,
Where the shadow falls the deepest,
Where the clustering nuts fall free —
That's the way for Billy and me.

There let us walk, there let us play,
Through the meadows, among the hay,
Up the water, and o'er the lea —
That's the way for Billy and me.

James Hogg

Poetry *Bed In Summer* by R. L. Stevenson, *Going Barefoot* by Judith Thurman,
Extra *Rain In Summer* by H. W. Longfellow.

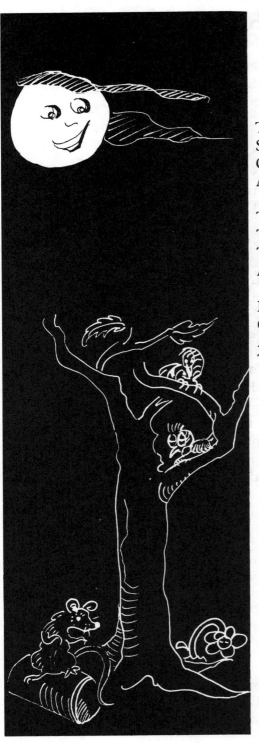

The Moon

The moon has a face like the clock in the hall;
She shines on thieves on the garden wall,
On streets and fields and harbour quays,
And birdies asleep in the forks of the trees.

The squalling cat and the squeaking mouse,
The howling dog by the door of the house,
The bat that lies in bed at noon,
All love to be out by the light of the moon.

But all the things that belong to the day
Cuddle to sleep to be out of her way;
And flowers and children close their eyes
Till up in the morning the sun shall arise.

Robert Louis Stevenson

1. How is the moon's face like the clock in the hall?
2. Name three people on whom the moon shines.
3. Name three animals on whom the moon shines.
4. Where would you find the bat at noon, do you think?
5. Make a list of five moon-words, e.g. *moonlight, moonbuggy.*

1. Make up your own moon-shaped poem. Here is an example:

PALE FACE
DON'T STARE AT ME
YOU ARE WHITE
AND
SCARY
NOW I AM
PALE FACE TOO

2. Can you name the Moonchester United players? Here are two — *Trevor Moonphy* and *Johnny Moonman*. Make up names for the other nine.

Make crayon rubbings, using cardboard stencils of the moon, trees, cat, dog, etc.

Listen to *Clair de Lune* by Debussy.

Poetry Extra Read *The Night* by James Stephens, *Is the Moon Tired?* by Christina Rossetti, *Flying* by J. M. Westrup.

There Came a Day

There came a day that caught the summer
Wrung its neck
Plucked it
And ate it.

Now what shall I do with the trees?
The day said, the day said.
Strip them bare, strip them bare.
Let's see what is really there.

And what shall I do with the sun?
The day said, the day said.
Roll him away till he's cold and small.
He'll come back rested if he comes back at all.

And what shall I do with the birds?
The day said, the day said.
The birds I've frightened, let them flit,
I'll hang out pork for the brave tomtit.

And what shall I do with the seed?
The day said, the day said.
Bury it deep, see what it's worth.
See if it can stand the earth.

What shall I do with the people?
The day said, the day said.
Stuff them with apple and blackberry pie —
They'll love me then till the day they die.

There came this day and he was autumn.
His mouth was wide
And red as a sunset.
His tail was an icicle.

Ted Hughes

ROUND THE CORNER,
PAST THE WALL

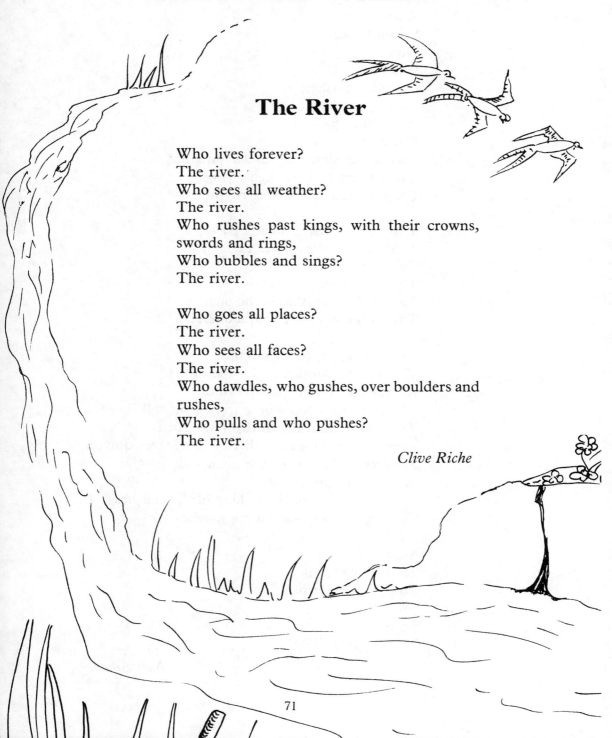

The River

Who lives forever?
The river.
Who sees all weather?
The river.
Who rushes past kings, with their crowns,
swords and rings,
Who bubbles and sings?
The river.

Who goes all places?
The river.
Who sees all faces?
The river.
Who dawdles, who gushes, over boulders and
rushes,
Who pulls and who pushes?
The river.

Clive Riche

The Song the Train Sang

Now
When
Steam hisses;
Now
When the
Coupling clashes;
Now
When the
Wind rushes
Comes the slow but sudden swaying,
Every truck and carriage trying
For a smooth and better rhythm.

This... is... the... one...
That... is... the... one...
This is the one,
That is the one,
This is the one, that is the one,
This is the one, that is the one...

Over the river, past the mill,
Through the tunnel under the hill;
Round the corner, past the wall,
Through the wood where trees grow tall.
Then in sight of the town by the river,
Brake by the crossing where white leaves quiver.
Slow as the streets of the town slide past
And the windows stare
                     at the jerking of the coaches
Coming into the station approaches.

Stop at the front.
Stop at the front.
Stop... at the front.
Stop... at the...
Stop.
        AHHHHH!

Neil Adams

1. How many train-sounds can you find in the poem?
2. Which words in the poem refer to:
   (a) *moving to and fro*
   (b) *the sound steam makes*
   (c) *metal striking against metal*
   (d) *gentle and even*
   (e) *tremble and shiver*
3. Make up train-words of your own.
   e.g. *trainthunder, trainsmoking*
4. Draw a picture of a train in your copy and write a NO-Poem inside it.
   Here is an example.

> *Train*
> *rushes past*
> *blowing smoke*
> *whistle screams*
> *wheels clatter*
> **NO** *tracks!*

1. Make a 'sticky paper' picture, using rectangles for the train carriages. Paste on cut-outs of the other items mentioned in the poem. Paste on light-coloured squares as train-windows, and draw faces on them.
2. Make a tape recording of a train journey using sounds and effects created by the children in the class.

Poetry Extra *The Train to Glasgow* by Wilma Horsbrugh, *The Song of the Engine* by H. Worsley-Benison. *The Train and the Hill* (anon). *The Engine Driver* by Clive Sansom

Noise

I like noise.
The whoop of a boy, the thud of a hoof,
The rattle of rain on a galvanized roof,
The hubbub of traffic, the roar of a train,
The throb of machinery numbing the brain,
The switching of wires in an overhead tram,
The rush of the wind, a door on the slam,
The boom of thunder, the crash of the waves,
The din of a river that races and raves,
The crack of a rifle, the clank of a pail,
The strident tattoo of a swift-slapping sail —
From any old sound that the silence destroys
Arises a gamut of soul-stirring joys.
I like noise.

J. Pope

1   Make your own Sound Chart.

LOUD	SOFT
1. electric drill	1. cat purring
2.	2.
3.	3.
4.	4.
5.	5.

2. Play the *Sound-Guessing Game*. Tape some familiar sounds around the house, e.g. water boiling, tea pouring, doors closing, and replay them in class. Whoever recognizes all the sounds wins the game.

Poetry Extra   *Circles* by John Kershaw, *The Roundabout* by Clive Sansom, *Engineers* by Jimmy Garthwaite, *Village Sounds* by James Reeves *Noise* by A. A. Milne.

Rainy Nights

I like the town on rainy nights
   When everything is wet —
When all the town has magic lights
   And streets of shining jet!

When all the rain about the town
   Is like a looking-glass,
And all the lights are upside down
   Below me as I pass.

In all the pools are velvet skies,
   And down the dazzling street
A fairy city gleams and lies
   In beauty at my feet.

Irene Thompson

The Spinning Earth

The earth, they say,
spins round and round.
It doesn't look it
from the ground,
and never makes
a spinning sound.

And water never
swirls and swishes
from oceans full
of dizzy fishes,
and shelves don't lose
their pans and dishes.

And houses don't go whirling by
or puppies swirl around the sky.
or robins spin instead of fly.

It may be true
what people say
about one spinning
night and day...
But I keep wondering, anyway.

Aileen Fisher

Television Aerials

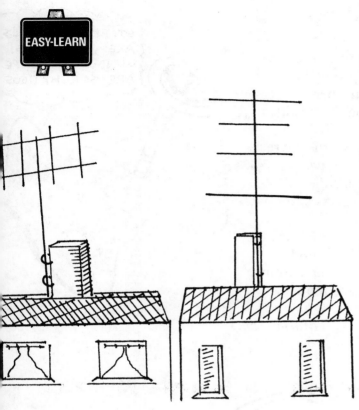

Television aerials
Look like witches' brooms.
When they finish flying
They leave them on the roof

Television aerials
Are sticks to prod the sky
To make clouds full of rain
Hurry by.

Television aerials
Reach above chimney tops
To make a perch
Where tired birds can stop.

Television aerials
Are fixed to the chimney side
To rake us songs and pictures
Out of the sky.

Stanley Cook

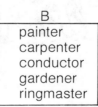 Join each object in A to the person who uses it in B.

A	B
baton	painter
trowel	carpenter
whip	conductor
hammer	gardener
paintbrush	ringmaster

 Make models of houses with television aerials, using very thin copper wire or pipe cleaners.

Poetry *Rainy Nights* by Irene Thompson, *Pylons* by Keith Bosley, *I Wonder* by
Extra Jeannie Kirby.

Carbreakers

There's a graveyard in our street,
But it's not for putting people in;
The bodies that they bury here
Are made of steel and paint and tin.

The people come and leave their wrecks
For crunching in the giant jaws
Of a great hungry car-machine,
That lives on bonnets, wheels and doors.

When I pass by the yard at night,
I sometimes think I hear a sound
Of ghostly horns that moan and whine,
Upon that metal-graveyard mound.

Marion Lines

 Using cardboard boxes and other waste materials, construct models of cars. Paint and decorate your models

---

Poetry *Chant of the Awakening Bulldozers* by Patricia Hubbell, *House Coming*
Extra *Down* by Eleanor Farjeon, *House Moving* by Patricia Hubbell, *Steam Shovel* by Charles Malam.

The Old Field

The old field is sad
Now the children have gone home.
They have played with him all afternoon,
Kicking the ball to him, and him
Kicking it back.

But now it is growing cold and dark.
He thinks of their warm breath, and their
Feet like little hot-water bottles.
A bit rough, some of them, but still . . .

And now, he thinks, there's not even a dog
To tickle me.
The gates are locked.
The birds don't like this nasty sneaking wind,
And nor does he.

D. J. Enright

1. Describe how it feels to:
    (a) walk barefoot on grass
    (b) paddle in mud
    (c) roll a snowball in your hand
    (d) suck an ice cube
    (e) hold a caterpillar

2. Complete each sentence with the correct word from the box.

    (a) *Grass is the field's*
    (b) *Soil is the field's*
    (c) *Leaves are the tree's*
    (d) *Branches are the tree's*
    (e) *Water is the river's*

| blood |
| feathers |
| hair |
| skin |
| fingers |

3. Draw a gate in your copy and write a list of five sad words on it.

Make a wall-collage based on the poem. Use thin strips of tissue paper as grass, and cut-out shapes to represent the children and ball etc. A wall may be made using tiny pebbles.

Poetry *The Hills* by Rachel Field, *Building Site* by Marian Lines, *The Wood of*
Extra *Flowers* by James Stephens *The Song of the Grass* by Leigh Hunt.

Where Go The Boats?

Dark brown is the river,
　Golden is the sand,
It flows along for ever,
　With trees on either hand.

Green leaves a-floating,
　Castles of the foam,
Boats of mine a-boating —
　Where will all come home?

On goes the river
　And out past the mill,
Away down the valley,
　Away down the hill.

Away down the river,
　A hundred miles or more,
Other little children
　Shall bring my boats ashore.

Robert Louis Stevenson

MIST AND MOONLIGHT

John Mouldy

I spied John Mouldy in his cellar,
Deep down twenty steps of stone;
In the dusk he sat a-smiling,
  Smiling there alone.

He read no book, he snuffed no candle;
The rats ran in, the rats ran out;
And far and near, the drip of water
  Went whisp'ring about.

The dusk was still, with dew a-falling,
I saw the Dog-star bleak and grim,
I saw a slim brown rat of Norway
  Creep over him.

I spied John Mouldy in his cellar,
Deep down twenty steps of stone;
In the dusk he sat a-smiling,
  Smiling there alone.

Walter de la Mare

Windy Nights

Whenever the moon and stars are set,
    Whenever the wind is high,
All night long in the dark and wet,
    A man goes riding by.
Late in the night when the fires are out,
Why does he gallop and gallop about?

Whenever the trees are crying aloud,
    And ships are tossed at sea,
By, on the highway, low and loud,
    By at the gallop goes he.
By at the gallop he goes, and then
By he comes back at the gallop again.

Robert Louis Stevenson

1. Why does the horseman gallop about on wet and windy nights?
2. How do we know that he never stops for a rest?
3. At what time of year would you be certain to see him?
4. Name three things the horseman might be wearing.
5. Do cars travel on the highway?
6. Which two words describe the sound made by the wind?
7. Why do you think this horseman might be a ghost?

Write a poem about a man who can't stop breaking the *Rules of the Road*. Begin like this:

> *Whenever the traffic lights are red,*
> *Whenever the sign says STOP!....*

Cut out cardboard stencils of the horse and rider, the moon, trees etc. The stencils may be placed on a sheet of paper to form a design. The surrounding area is spattered with a watery paint using a soft brush, a sponge or a toothbrush.

Listen to the *Light Cavalry Overture* by Franz Von Suppé.

Poetry
Extra
The Horseman by Walter de la Mare, *The Six Badgers* by Robert Graves, *The Flying Dutchman* by Charles Godfrey Leland. *The Spunky* (Anon).

Nightening

When you wake up at night
and it's dark and frightening,
don't be afraid —
turn on the lightening.

Michael Dugan

The Goblin

There's a goblin as green
As a goblin can be
Who is sitting outside
And is waiting for me.

When he knocked on my door
And said softly, 'Come play.'
I answered, 'No thank you,
Now, please, go away.'

But the goblin as green
As a goblin can be
Is still sitting outside
And is waiting for me.

Jack Prelutsky

Haunted House

There's a house upon the hilltop
We will not go inside
For that is where the witches live,
Where ghosts and goblins hide.

Tonight they have their party,
All the lights are burning bright,
But oh we will not go inside
The haunted house tonight.

The demons there are whirling
And the spirits swirl about.
They sing their songs to Hallowe'en
'Come join the fun,' they shout.

But we do not want to go there
So we run with all our might
And oh we will not go inside
The haunted house tonight.

Jack Prelutsky

1. Name all the frightening creatures that live in the haunted house.
2. Why are they holding their party?
3. Complete the following sentences:
   'I want a bat-and-toadstool sandwich!', said Wanda Witch.
   'I want a .... ice cream!', said Gus Goblin.
   'I want a .... milkshake!', said Dan the Demon
4. Write down five words that rhyme with 'witch'.
5. When will the party end?
6. What present would *you* bring to the party if you were invited?

1. List five telephone numbers from a goblin telephone directory,
   e.g. *Gloomtown 9999.*
2. Make up your own poem about a witch. Begin like this:

> *Wanda Witch is such a puzzle,*
> *She loves to chomp and chew and guzzle*
> *Tons of chocolate, bags of sweets....*

1. Do a charcoal drawing of the haunted house.
2. Make Hallowe'en masks using large paper bags, sheets of cartridge paper, old cardboard boxes etc. You will need a scissors, paper plates and paint or crayons.

Listen to *Night on a Bare Mountain* by Moussorgsky

EASY-LEARN

The Horseman

I heard a horseman
  Ride over the hill;
The moon shone clear,
  The night was still;
His helm was silver,
  And pale was he;
And the horse he rode
  Was of ivory.

Walter de la Mare

Poetry *The Man Who Wasn't There* by Brian Lee, *Green Candles* by Humbert
Extra Wolfe, *Queer Things* by James Reeves, *A Meeting* by George D. Painter.

In The Orchard

There was a giant by the Orchard Wall
Peeping about on this side and on that,
And feeling in the trees. He was as tall
As the big apple tree, and twice as fat:
His beard poked out, all bristly-black, and there
Were leaves and gorse and heather in his hair.

He held a blackthorn club in his right hand,
And plunged the other into every tree,
Searching for something — You could stand
Beside him and not reach up to his knee,
So big he was — I trembled lest he should
Come trampling, round-eyed, down to where I stood.

I tried to get away. — But, as I slid
Under a bush, he saw me, and he bent
Down deep at me, and said, *'Where is she hid?'*
I pointed over there, and off he went —

But, while he searched, I turned and simply flew
Round by the lilac bushes back to you.

James Stephen.

1. Who is speaking in the poem?
2. How tall was the giant?
3. Why was he looking for the girl?
4. Was the giant real or imagined?
5. Write a description of the giant's beard.
6. Complete the following phrases:
    (a) as tall as a......
    (b) as skinny as a....
    (c) as sweet as a.....
    (d) as cold as a......

1. Use the Giant Steps to make words that describe a giant.

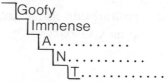

2. Make up your own tongue twister. Begin like this:
Jealous giants jog.....

Make a felt-and-fabric collage of a giant using scraps of felt and other materials such as cotton, tweed, leather, nylon, velvet etc.

Listen to 'In the Hall of the Mountain King' from *Peer Gynt* by Grieg.

A Short Litany

From witches and wizards and longtail'd buzzards,
And creeping things that run in hedge bottoms,
Good Lord deliver us.

Traditional

Poetry *Bellowed the Ogre* by Lilian Moore, *A Giant Named Stanley,* by Michael
Extra   Patrick Hearn, *Toodley Gronickpet: the goblin bagpiper* by Spike Milligan.

Midnight Wood

Dark in the wood the shadows stir:
　What do you see? –
Mist and moonlight, star and cloud,
Hunchback shapes that creep and crowd
　From tree to tree.

Dark in the wood a thin wind calls:
　What do you hear?
Frond and fern and clutching grass
Snigger at you as you pass,
　Whispering fear.

Dark in the wood a river flows:
　What does it hide? –
Otter, water-rat, old tin can,
Bones of fish and bones of a man
　Drift in its tide.

Dark in the wood the owlets shriek:
　What do they cry? –
Choose between the wood and river;
Who comes here is lost forever,
　And must die!

Raymond Wilson

1. Why is the poem called Midnight Wood?
2. What would hunchback shapes look like?
3. Can you find three words to describe the sound of the wind?
4. What does the clutching grass say to you as you pass?
5. Name five horrible insects you would find in Midnight Wood, e.g. the *Pepsi Blood-Spider*.
6. Make up your own title for this poem.

1. What does the Milk-Monster hide in its nest? — yogurt cartons, bottle tops? Make your own list.
2. The *Wolfrobin*, the *Shadowsparrow* and the *Haunting Crow* all live in Midnight Wood. Draw a picture of each bird.

Do a wet-sheet painting based on this poem. A sheet of duplicating paper is painted over using clean water and a brush. A sponge or cloth may also be used to dampen the paper. Paint the picture on top of this.

Listen to *'Danse Macabre'* by Saint-Saens.

Moths and Moonshine

Moths and moonshine mean to me
Magic — madness — mystery.
Witches dancing weird and wild
Mischief make for man and child.
Owls screech from woodland shades,
Moths glide through moonlit glades
Moving in dark and secret wise
Like a plotter in disguise.
Moths and moonshine mean to me
Magic — madness — mystery.

James Reeves

Poetry Extra *Old Shellover,* by Walter de la Mare, *Hist Whist* by e. e. cummings, *The Mewlips* by J. R. R. Tolkien, *Little Boy Lost* by Stevie Smith.

The Visitor

A crumbling churchyard, the sea and the moon;
The waves had gouged out grave and bone;
A man was walking, late and alone...

He saw a skeleton on the ground;
A ring on a bony finger he found.

He ran home to his wife and gave her the ring.
'Oh, where did you get it?' He said not a thing.

'It's the loveliest ring in the world,' she said,
As it glowed on her finger. They slipped off to bed.

At midnight they woke. In the dark outside,
'Give me my ring!' a chill voice cried.

'What was that, William? What did it say?'
'Don't worry, my dear. It'll soon go away.'

'I'm coming!' A skeleton opened the door.
'Give me my ring!' It was crossing the floor.

'What was that, William? What did it say?'
'Don't worry, my dear. It'll soon go away.'

'I'm reaching you now! I'm climbing the bed.'
The wife pulled the sheet right over her head.

It was torn from her grasp and tossed in the air;
'I'll drag you out of bed by the hair!'

'What was that, William? What did it say?'
'Throw the ring through the window! THROW IT AWAY!'

She threw it. The skeleton leapt from the sill,
Scooped up the ring and clattered downhill,
Fainter... and fainter... Then all was still.

Ian Serraillier

1. Where was the churchyard?
2. How do you know that the churchyard was old?
3. Why was the man walking there *late and alone*?
4. Who was more frightened, William or his wife?
5. What would have happened if William's wife had kept the ring?
6. Where did the skeleton go to after it had clattered off downhill?
7. Make up your own title for the poem.

1. You have invented a toothpaste for skeletons which you call *Deadly White*, Write a slogan to sell the toothpaste. Begin like this:
   For a really spine-tingling smile....
2. Longbone and the Wailers, the skeleton pop-group, have just released their third record. It is called *I'm Dyin' to See You.*
   Think up possible titles for their first two records.

Make up your own *Dance of the Skeletons* using castanets or coconut shells. Children might mime the movements of the skeleton dancers.

The Hidebehind

Have you seen the Hidebehind?
I don't think you will, mind you,
because as you're running through the dark
the Hidebehind's behind you.

Michael Rosen

Poetry *The Bogus-Boo* by James Reeves, *The Hairy Toe* (anon), *John Mouldy* by
Extra Walter de la Mare, *Tom Bone* by Charles Causley.

The Man Who Wasn't There

Yesterday upon the stair
I met a man who wasn't there;
He wasn't there again today,
I wish, I wish, he'd go away.

I've seen his shapeless shadow-coat
Beneath the stairway; hanging about;
And outside, muffled in a cloak
The same colour as the dark;

I've seen him in a black, black suit
Shaking, under the broken light;
I've seen him swim across the floor
And disappear beneath the door;

And once, I almost heard his breath
Behind me, running up the path;
Inside he leant against the wall,
And turned . . . and was no one at all.

Yesterday upon the stair
I met the man who wasn't there;
He wasn't there again today,
I wish, I wish, he'd go away.

Brian Lee

Witch Goes Shopping

Witch rides off
Upon her broom
Finds a space
To park it.
Takes a shiny shopping cart
Into the supermarket.
Smacks her lips and reads
The list of things she needs:

>'Six bats' wings
>Worms in brine
>Ears of toads
>Eight or nine.
>Slugs and bugs
>Snake skins dried
>Buzzard innards
>Pickled, fried.'

Witch takes herself
From shelf to shelf
Cackling all the while.
Up and down and up and down and
In and out each aisle.
Out come cans and cartons
Tumbling to the floor.
'This,' says Witch, now all a-twitch
'Is a crazy store.
I CAN'T FIND A SINGLE THING
I AM LOOKING FOR!'

Lilian Moore

1. Where did the witch park her broom?
2. How is she dressed, do you think?
3. List five gruesome vegetables the witch forgot to put on her list,
   e.g. Itching Onions.
4. Why did the witch become angry?
5. This witch is called Dame Eliza Deathrattle. Her five friends are waiting at
   her cottage. Could you give them suitable names?

Make up Dame Deathrattle's dinner menu.

Poetry *W is For Witch* by Eleanor Farjeon, *Wild Witches' Ball* by Jack Prelutsky,
Extra *Witches Menu* by Sonja Nikolay, *Mixed Brews* by Clive Sansom.

The Witch's Cat

'My magic is dead,' said the witch, 'I'm astounded
That people can fly to the moon and around it.
It used to be mine and the cat's till they found it.
My broomstick is draughty, I snivel with cold
As I ride to the stars. I'm painfully old,
      And so is my cat;
      But planet-and-space-ship,
      Rocket or race-ship
Never shall part me from that.'

She wrote an advertisement; 'Witch in a fix
Willing to part with the whole bag of tricks,
Going cheap at the price at eighteen and six.'
But no one was ready to empty his coffers
For out-of-date rubbish. There weren't any offers —
      Except for the cat.
      'But planet-and-space-ship,
      Rocket or race-ship
Never shall part me from that.'

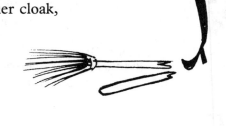

The tears trickled fast, not a sentence she spoke
As she stamped on her broom and the brittle stick broke,
And she dumped in a dustbin her hat and her cloak,
Then clean disappeared, leaving no prints;
And no one at all has set eyes on her since
      Or her tired old cat.
      'But planet-and-space-ship,
      Rocket or race-ship
Never shall part me from that.'

Ian Serraillier

1. Why is the witch surprised?
2. Why is her broomstick draughty?
3. What does she say about her cat?
4. Make a list of things the witch wished to sell.
5. What was the cat worth?
6. Why did the witch begin to cry?
7. What happened to the cat, do you think?

1. The witch's cat loved to catch moon-mice. What other moon-creatures did it catch?
2. Make up a witch's spell to turn the moon into ice-cream. Begin like this: *Frizzly lollipops, shivery jellies.....*

1. Make mobiles of the witch and the objects mentioned in the poem and hang them from a coathanger in the classroom.
2. Cut out witch, cat, bat etc. shapes using black cartridge paper and make a witch frieze.

Listen to *The Witch's Ride* from Hansel and Gretel by Humperdinck.

Poetry Extra   *The Ride-by-Nights* by Walter de la Mare, *Old Moll* by James Reeves, *The Witches' Ride'* by Karla Kuskin, *Two Witches* by Alexander Resnikoff.

Check

The Night was creeping on the ground!
She crept, and did not make a sound

Until she reached the tree: And then
She covered it, and stole again

Along the grass beside the wall!
— I heard the rustling of her shawl

As she threw blackness everywhere
Along the sky, the ground, the air,

And in the room where I was hid!
But, no matter what she did

To everything that was without,
She could not put my candle out!

So I stared at the Night! And she
Stared back solemnly at me!

James Stephens